Challenging
incredible puzzles

150+ timed puzzles to test your skill!

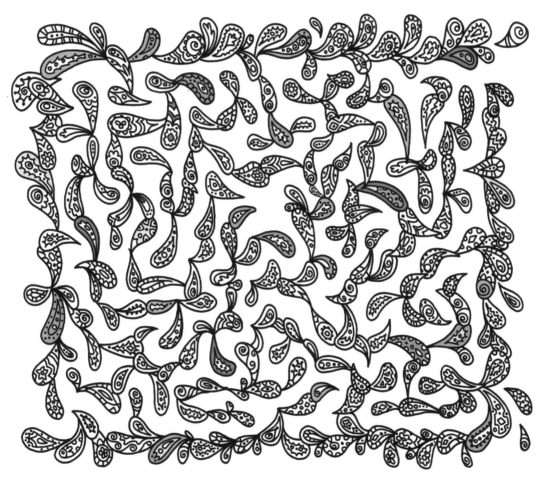

Illustrated by Giulia Lombardo, Marc Parchow,
Andrea Ebert, Lisa Mallet, Dani Cruz, Monica Bauleo,
Maria Neradova & Nicolae Negura
Written by Elizabeth Golding
Designed by Ben Potter & Anton Poitier

BARRON'S

First edition for the United States and Canada published
in 2018 by Barron's Educational Series, Inc.
First published in the U.K. by iSeek Ltd

This book was conceived, created, and
produced by iSeek Ltd
RH17 5QQ, UK

All inquiries should be addressed to:
Barron's Educational Series, Inc.
250 Wireless Boulevard
Hauppauge, New York 11788
www.barronseduc.com

ISBN: 978-1-4380-1207-0

Date of Manufacture: June 2018

Manufactured by: Ganboa, Andoain, Spain

Printed in Spain
9 8 7 6 5 4 3 2 1

Puzzle fun!

This book is jam-packed with amazing puzzles, which start easy and get harder as you go through the book. There are mazes, dot-to-dot, odd one out, spot the difference, and picture puzzles. Every puzzle has a time challenge at the top of the page. See if you can solve the puzzle faster and beat the challenge. Look out for this symbol:

BEAT THIS!

 Time challenge to beat.

The clock is in minutes and seconds. Use a watch with a second hand, or a cell phone timer, to check how long it takes to complete each puzzle. You can write down your time on each page.

Dot-to-dot

There is also a symbol on pages with dot-to-dot puzzles that tells you how many dots are in the puzzle, like this:

Spot the difference

Look out for this symbol for the spot the difference puzzles that tells you how many differences there are:

Double page dots

Some of the dot-to-dot puzzles go across the fold in the book. A few have different colored dots. Use different pencil colors to complete these puzzles.

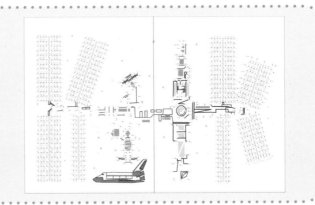

Solve and color!

Some of the puzzles can be colored, too. These are partially colored or blank, and you can complete the blank areas with colored pencils.

The solutions are at the end of the book, in case you get really stuck!

Only three shapes will fit the picture. Which ones?

BEAT THIS!
00:35

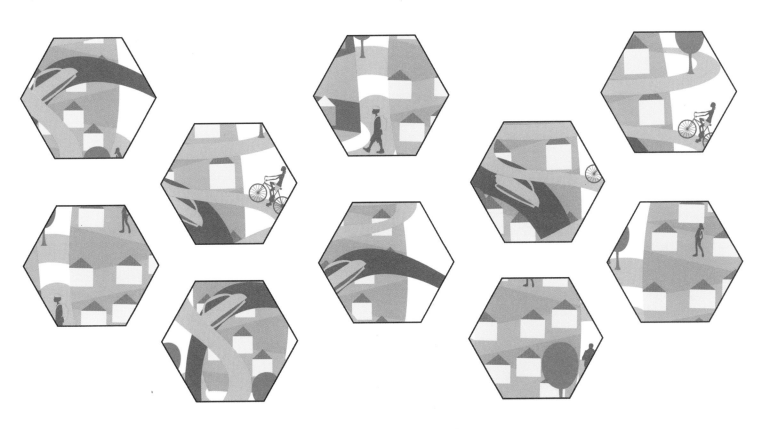

Find the hidden seal.

What a messy bedroom! Find your way across the floor.

BEAT THIS!
00:40

Find the pig with a square snout.

The wolf has blown down the pigs' little house. There is one unexpected item. Can you find it?

Wiggle your way from the top to the bottom!

Find the odd one out that you can eat.

One dog is different from the others. Which one?

BEAT THIS!
00:55

Help the ants feed their queen!

BEAT THIS!
00:55

Find the lost scarf.

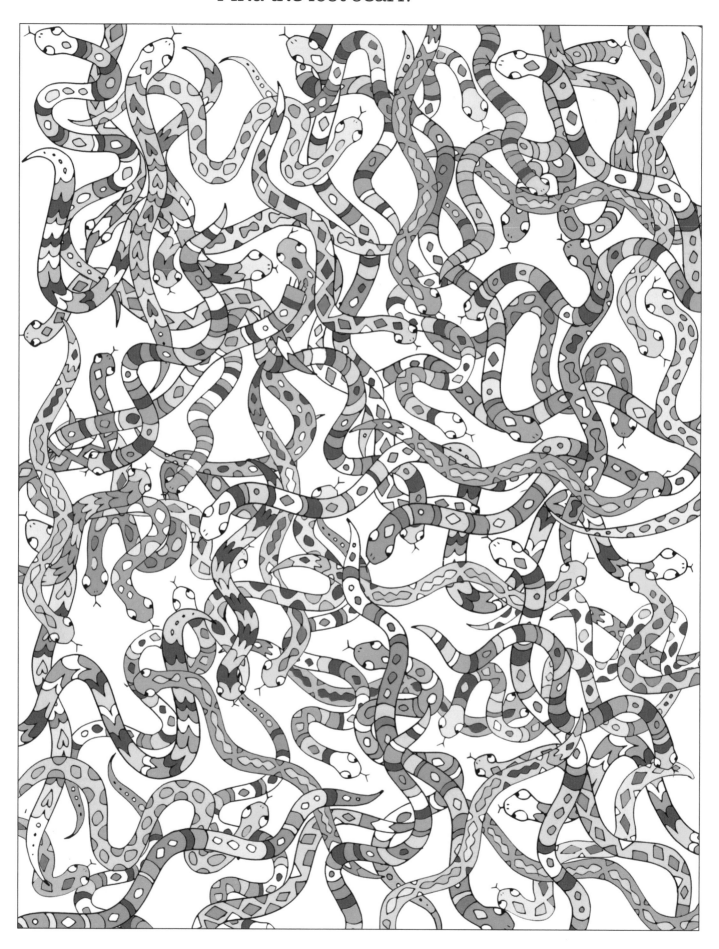

BEAT THIS!
00:55

Don't get trampled! Did you pass a yellow elephant?

Only two penguins, two crabs, and two seals are the same.
Which ones?

BEAT THIS!

00:55

It's okay, none of the snakes are poisonous, but be fast!

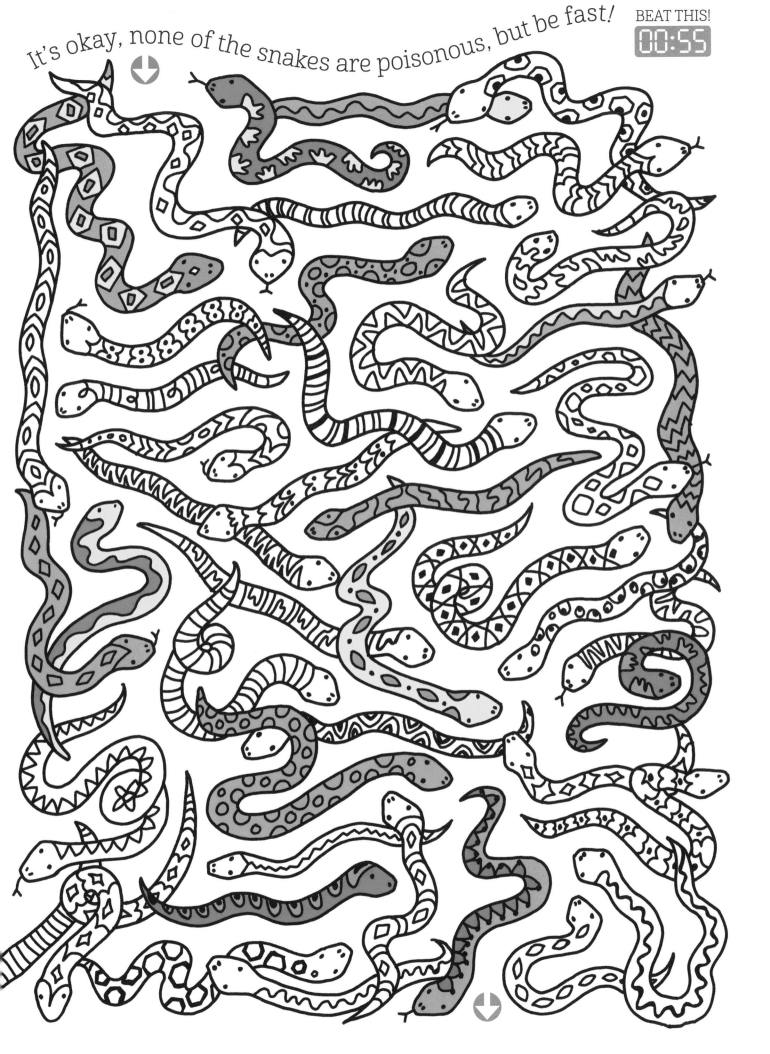

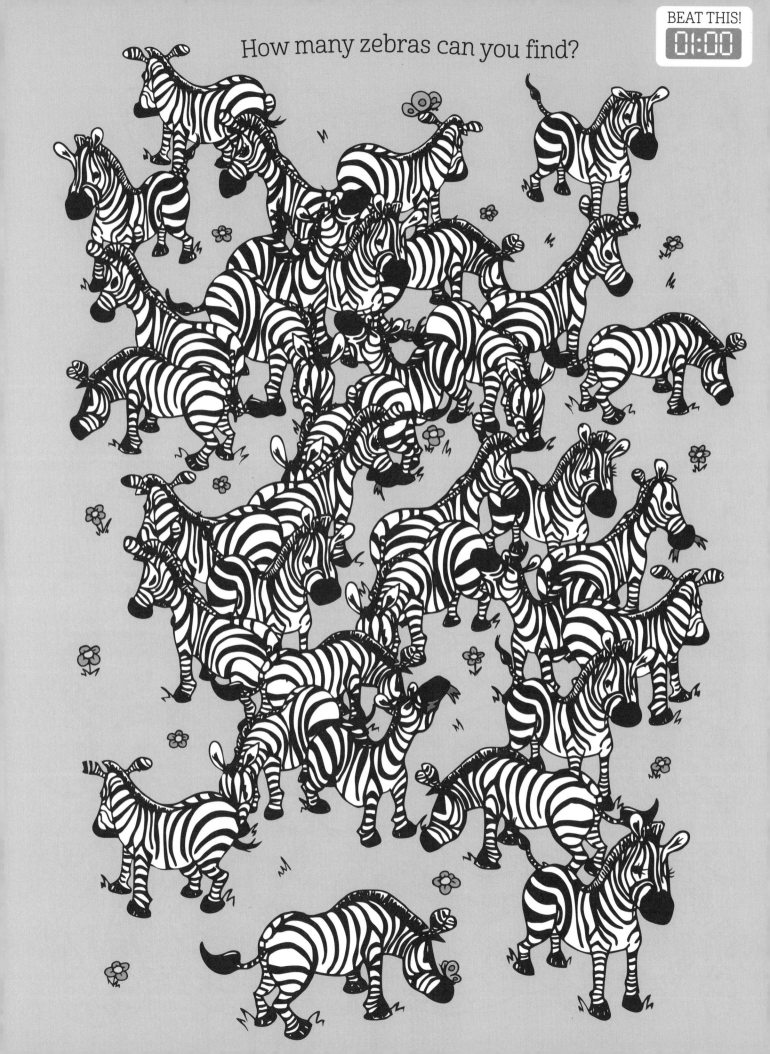

So many spots! Which one is the odd one out?

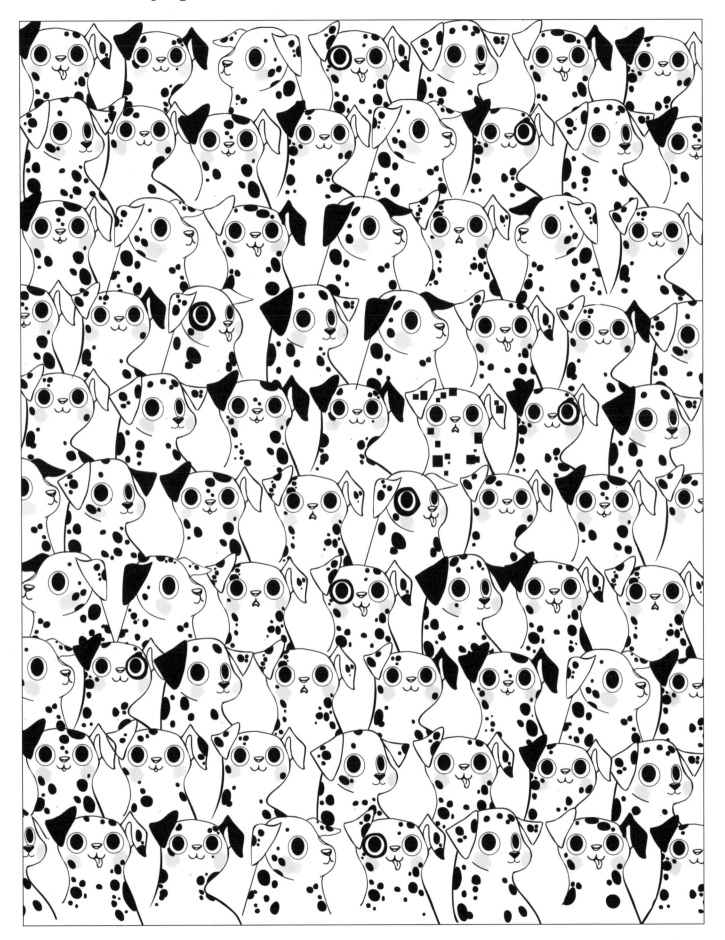

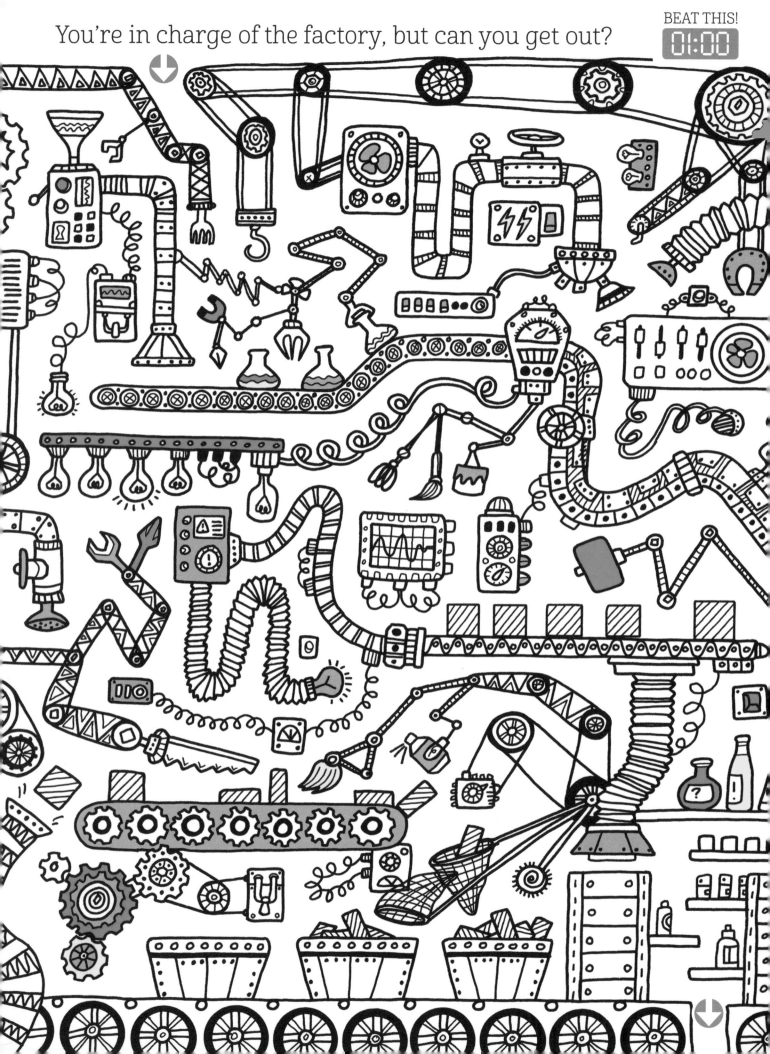

Are all of these really sunflowers? One is a bit odd.

Find the eggshells that match together.

Guide the rabbit home to his burrow.

BEAT THIS!
01:05

Which of these soccer balls is different from the rest?

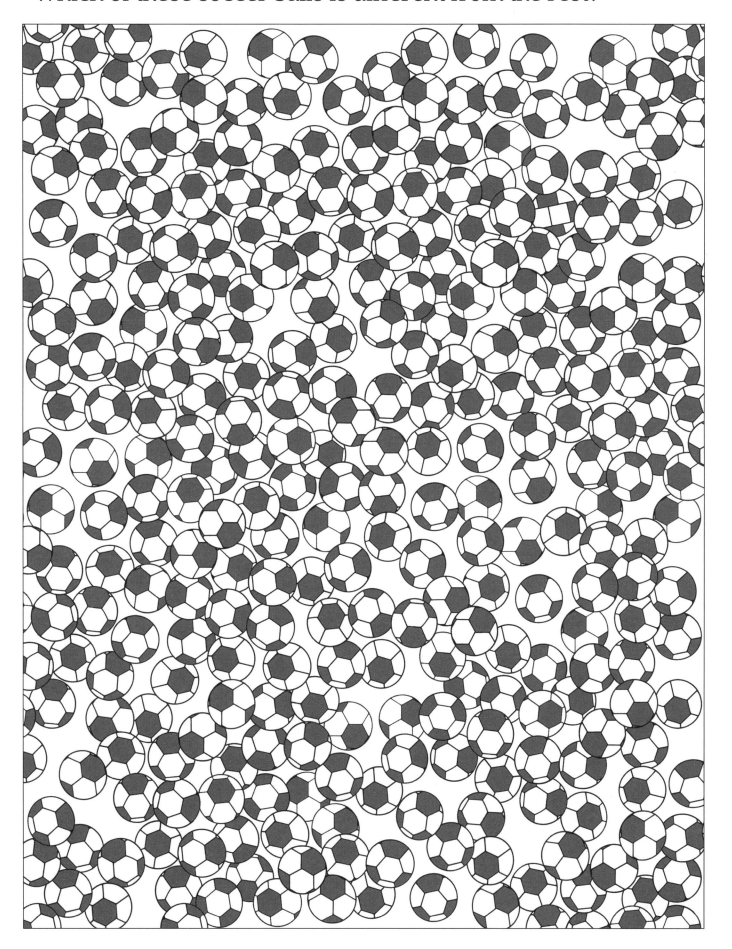

One of these men isn't a man. Which one?

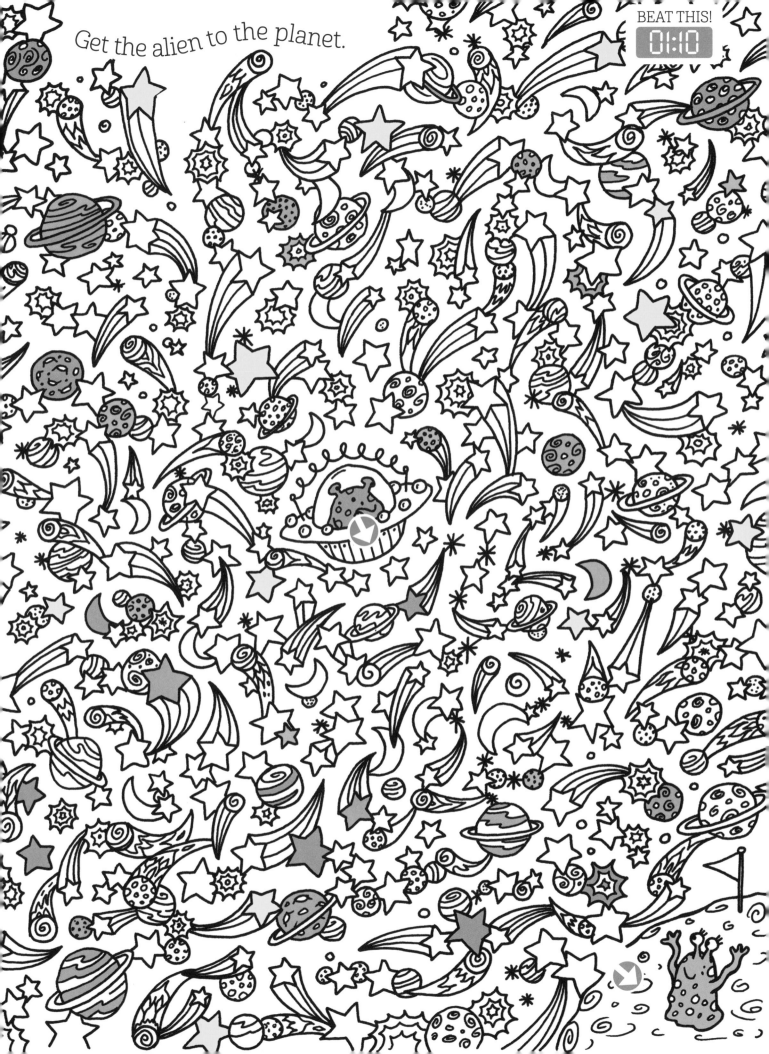

Get the alien to the planet.

One instrument is different from the rest. Which one?

Which pictures match what you can see in the two red circles?

All rabbits like carrots. Or do they?

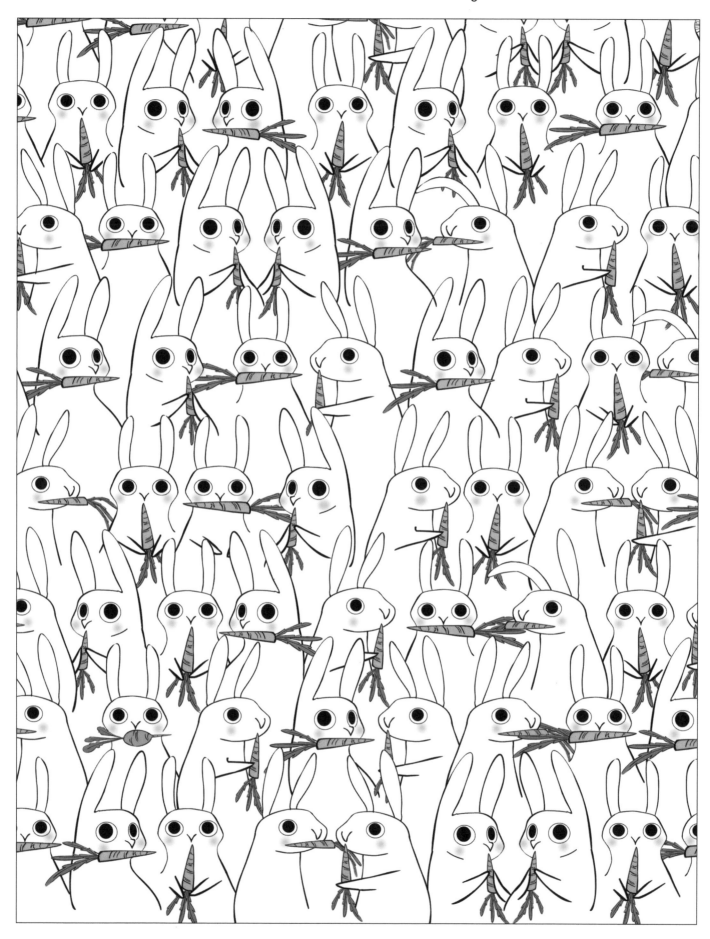

Only one plug is for the lamp. But which one?

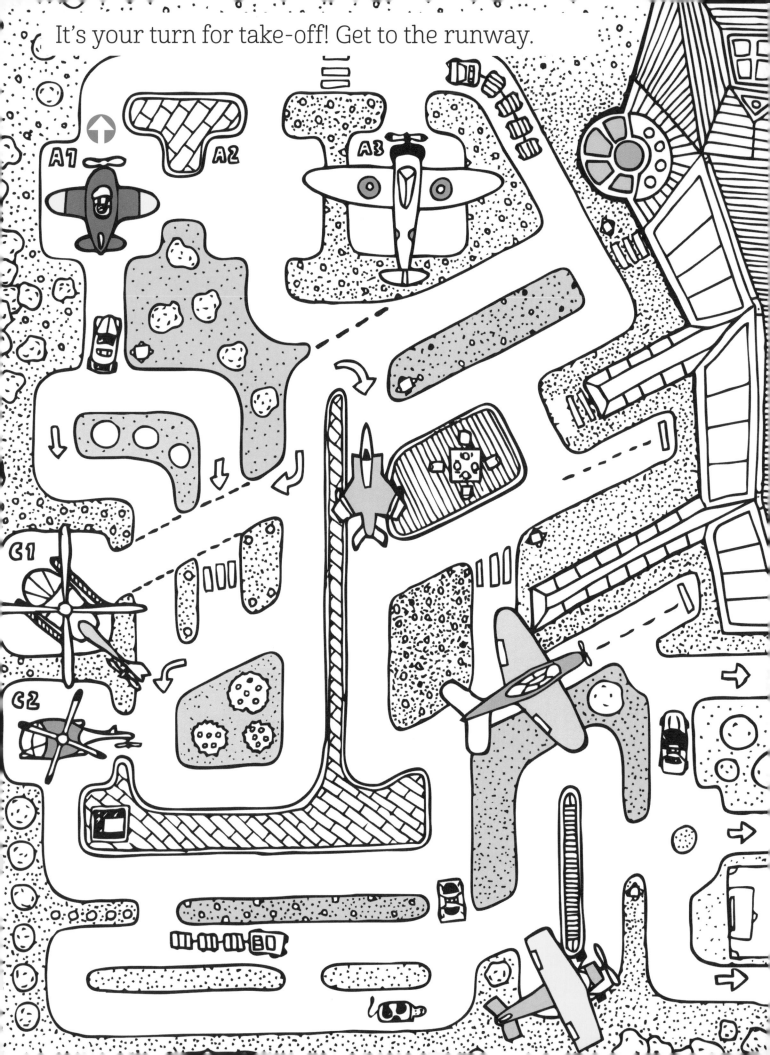

It's your turn for take-off! Get to the runway.

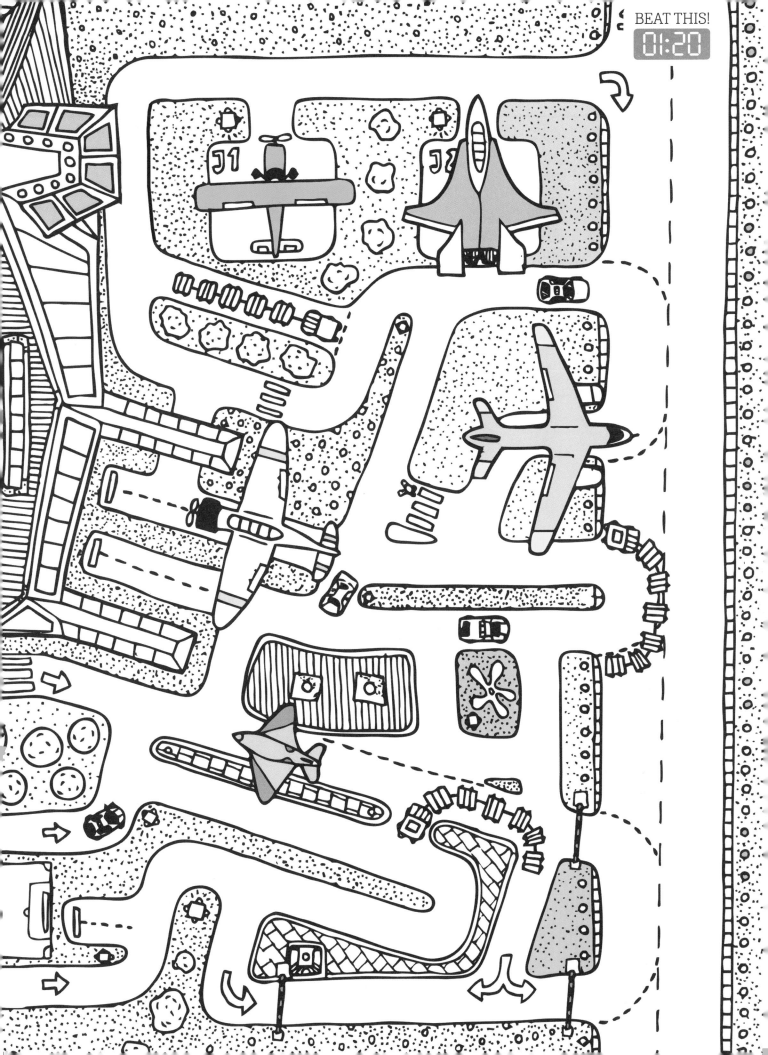

A mermaid seems to have joined the party. Circle her.

Match each dolphin to its shadow.

Which shadow belongs with which jumbled up picture?

Find your way through the fish's scales!

BEAT THIS!
01:30

Apart from the space referee, who is the odd one out?

Which piece of the puzzle is missing?

Find the 9 odd things on the beach or in the ocean.

BEAT THIS!
01:35

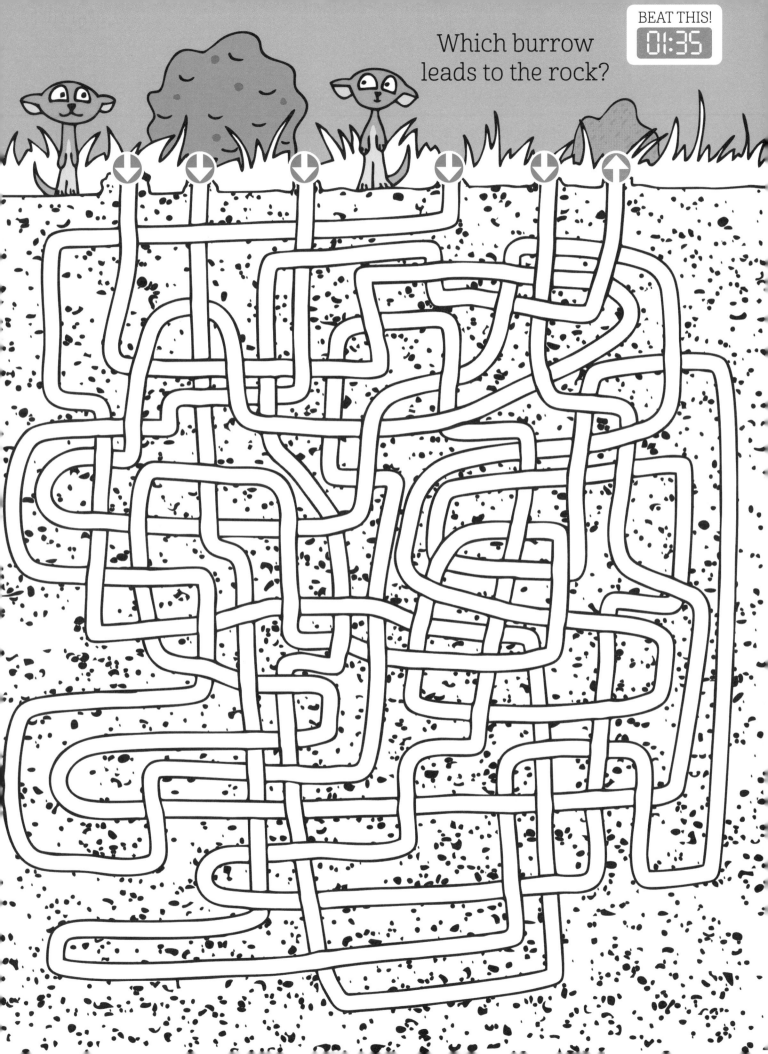

Which burrow leads to the rock?

BEAT THIS!
01:35

Find the pencil sharpened at both ends!

Tiptoe through the raindrops!

Find the flamingo standing on one leg.
Circle and color it pink!

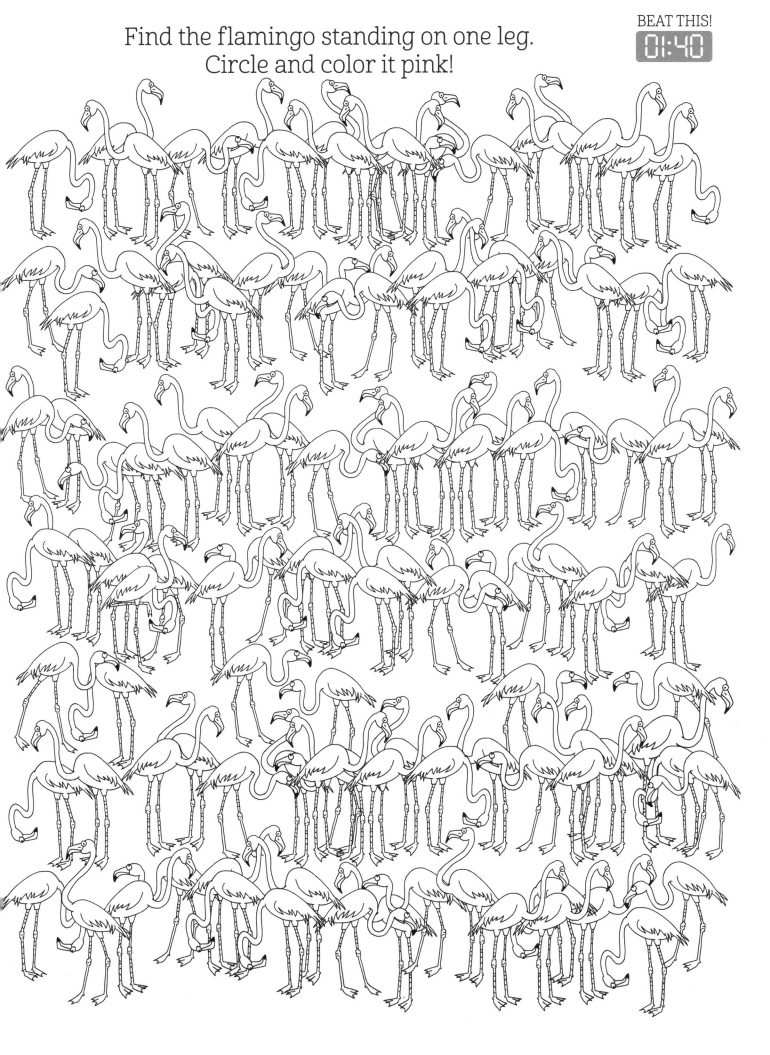

Get the hamster out the other end of the tubes!

You know who eats what! Who arrives first?

WINNER

Find the 12 things that don't belong in this room.

Which one of these cacti is different from the others?

How many skateboards can you find?

BEAT THIS!
01:55

Which bird is different from all the others?

How many starlings can you count?

One has something in its beak. Which one?

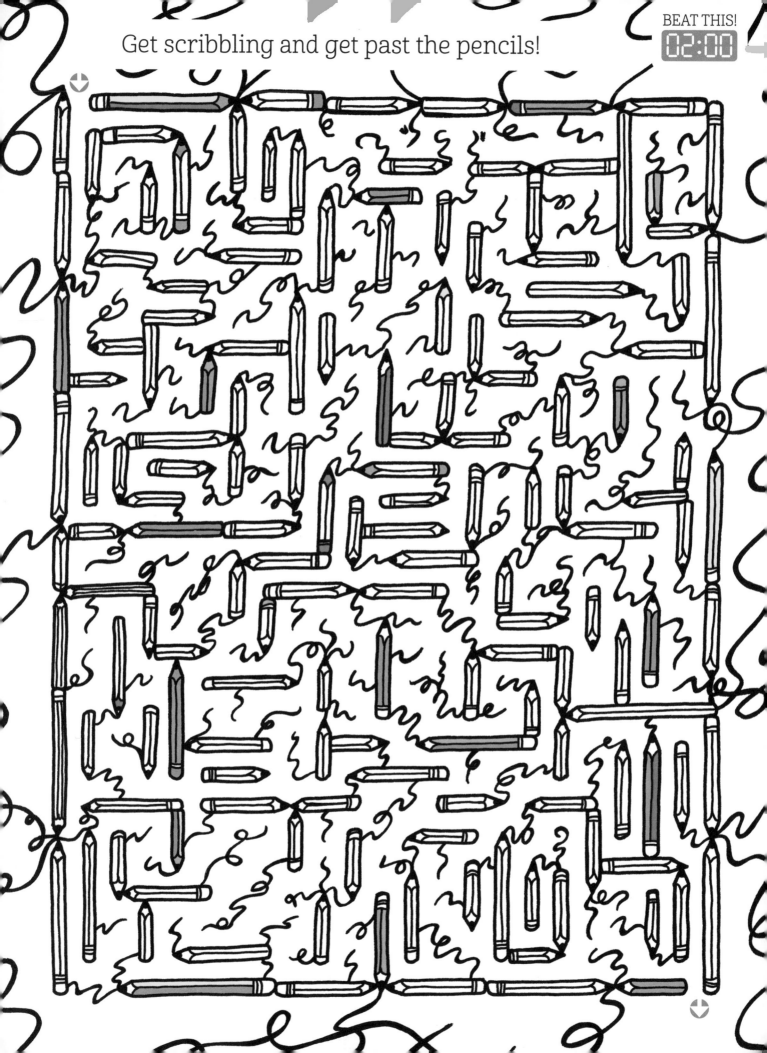

One elephant is different. Which one?

Try to find the teapot hiding among the teacups.

Only one set of colors has 9 different colors.
Which one?

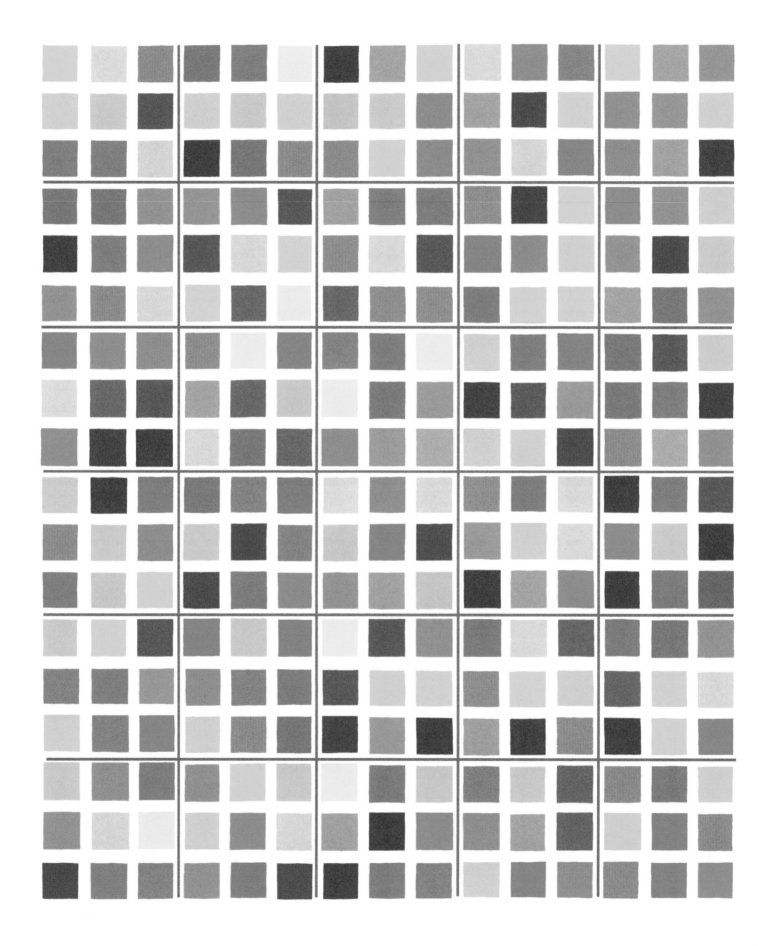

Find the 3 fruits that appear only once.

Katie has lost a button from her jacket.
Can you help her find it?

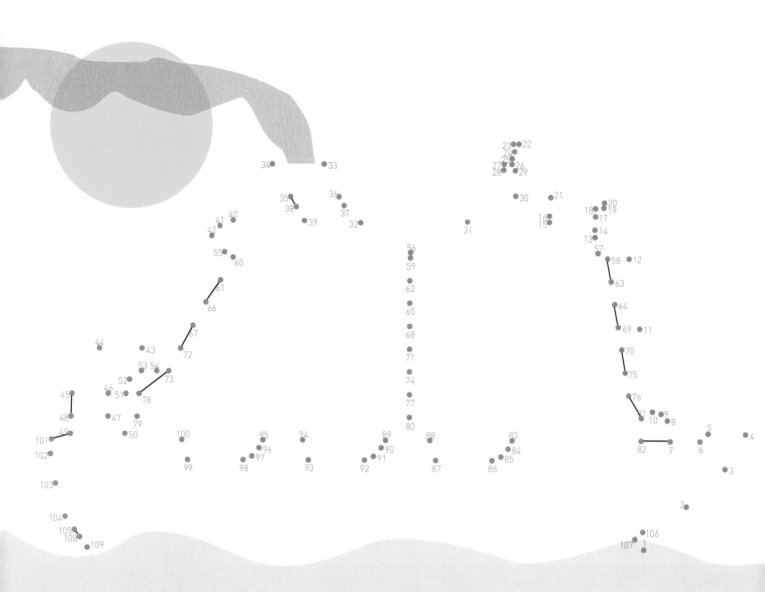

What is this? Connect the dots to find out!

Can you spot the differences?

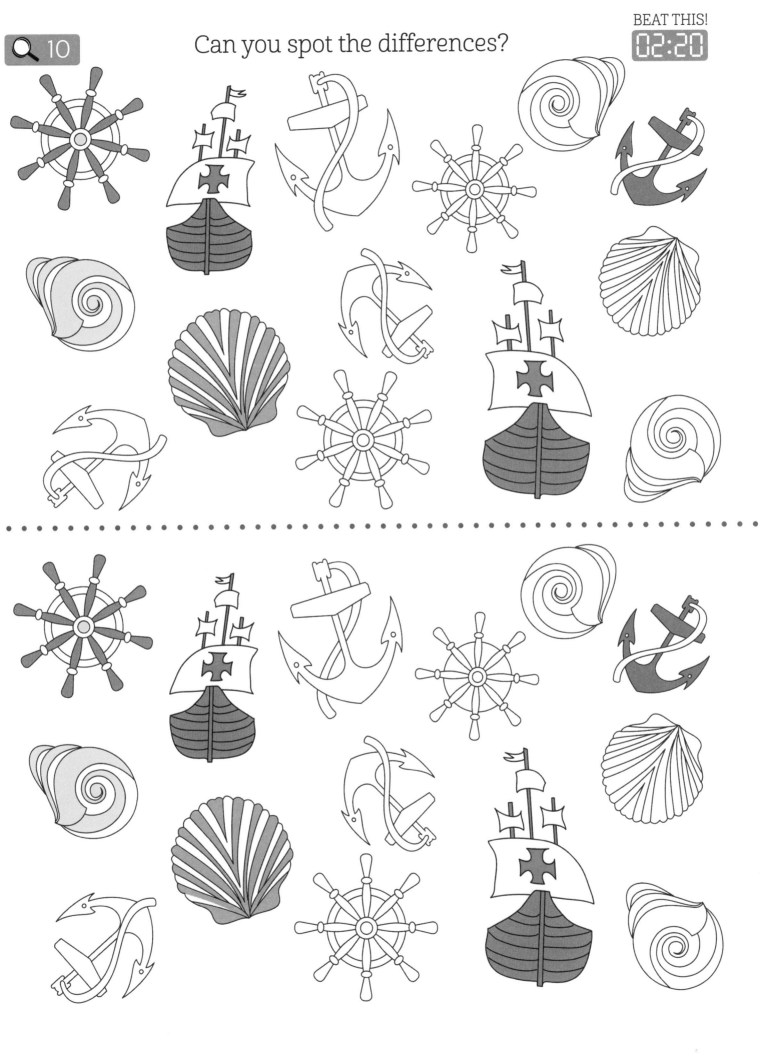

Get in the flow! Which ↓ way does the water go?

Connect the dots and add some more color to this!

Spot the differences.

Someone played a trick on the ghosts.
Which one doesn't belong?

Would you like to go in one of these?

Help the
crab get
to the sea!

How many stars can Sophie see from her window?

Circle the differences.

Connect the dots and add some more color to this!

Circle the differences.

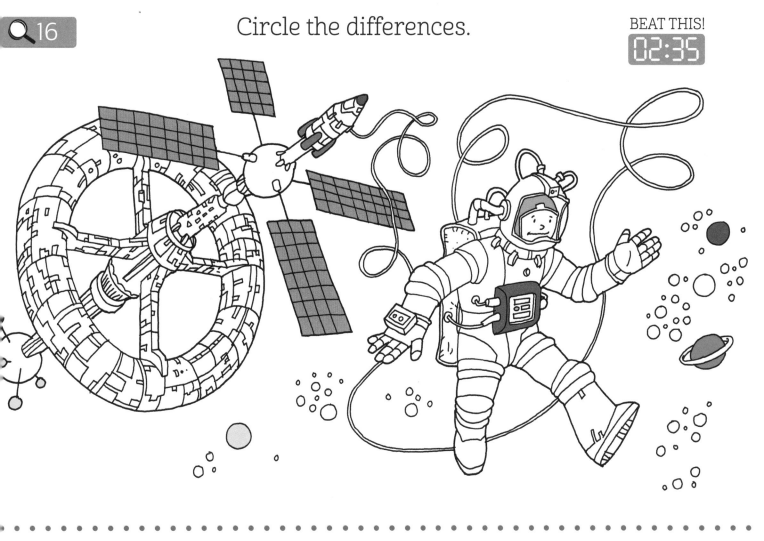

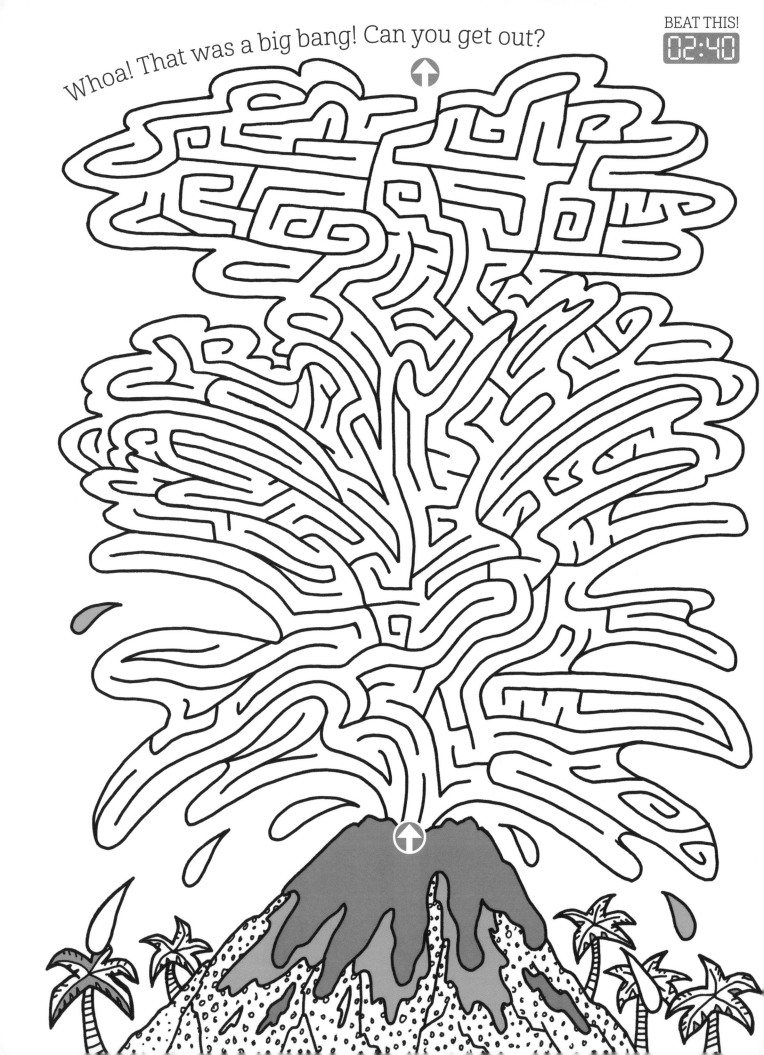

One of the cups is different from the rest. Which one?

Circle the differences.

Connect the dots and see what's leaping through the air.

How do you get from the front
door to the chimney?

One of these dogs is the odd one out, but which one?

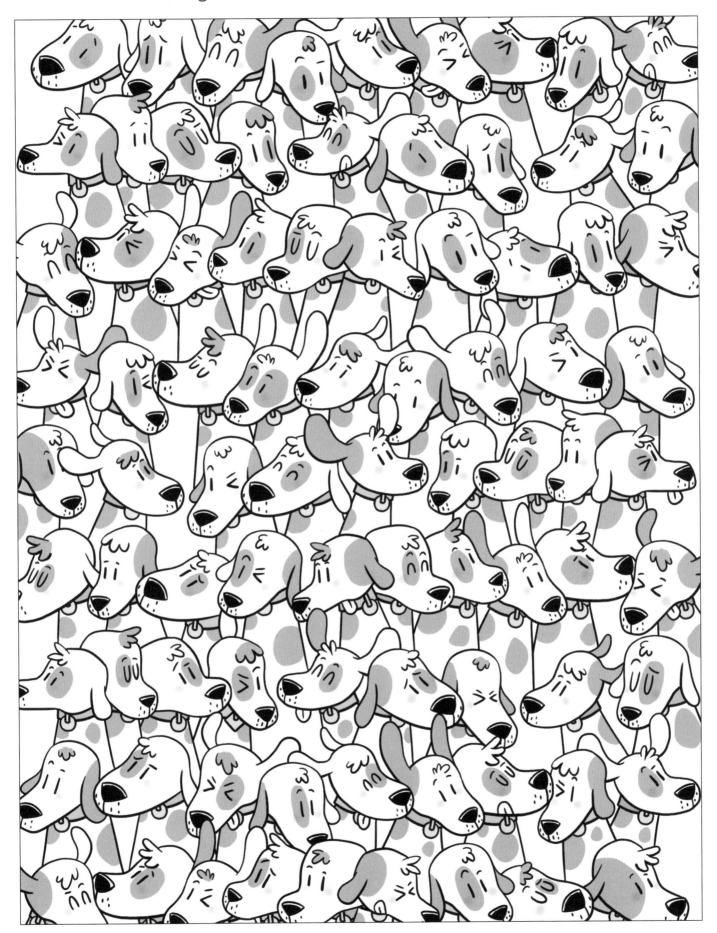

Connect the dots and add some color when you're done!

Four squares have 6 shapes in them.
Find them and beat the clock!

Spot the differences.

Find the snail that's waiting to be found. Color him in.

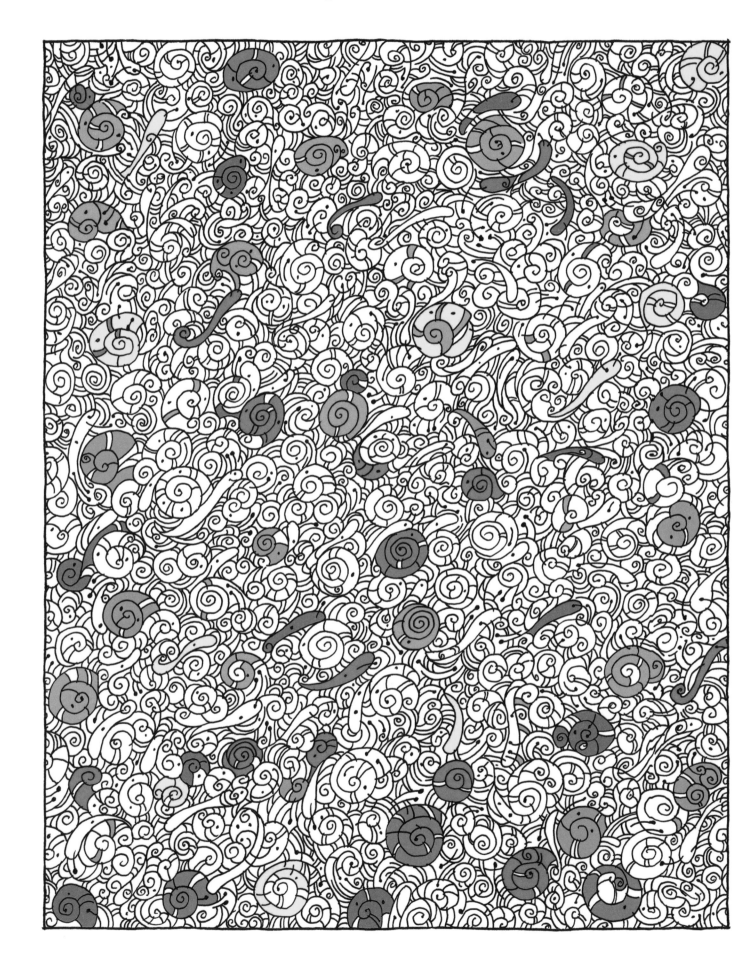

Connect the dots and take a great leap forward!

This building is impossible!
Find your way to one of the doors on this page.

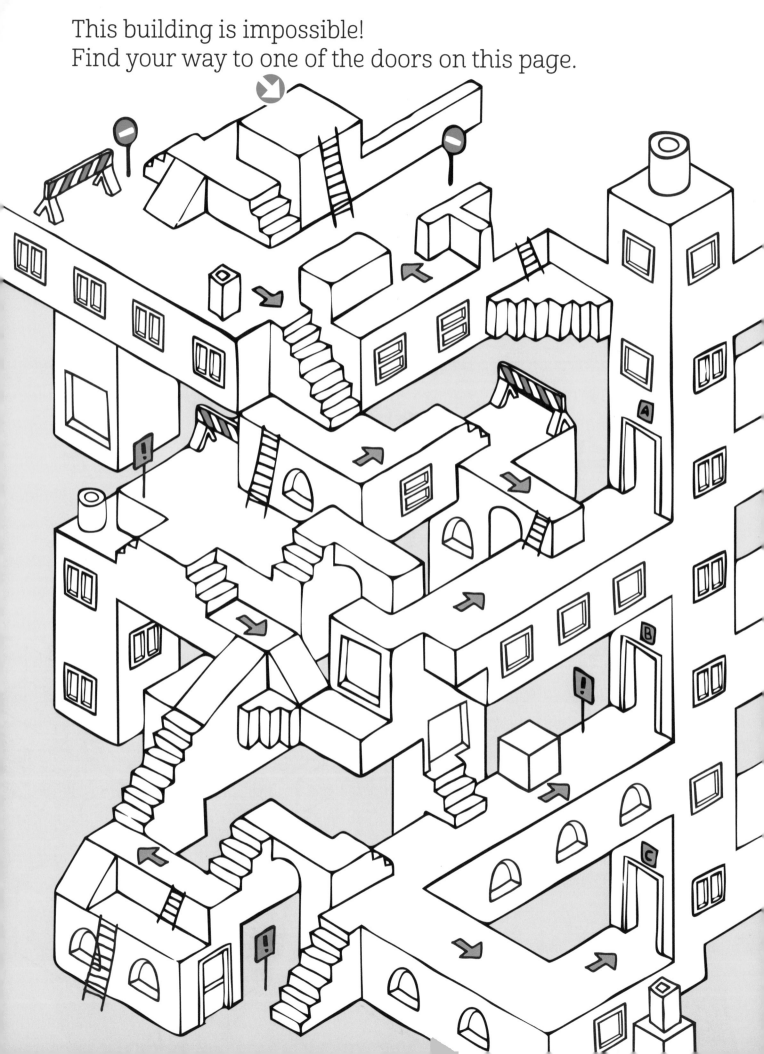

Found the right door? Only one of the doors on this page will lead you out of the maze!

Circle the differences.

These gingerbread men are all pairs, except one.

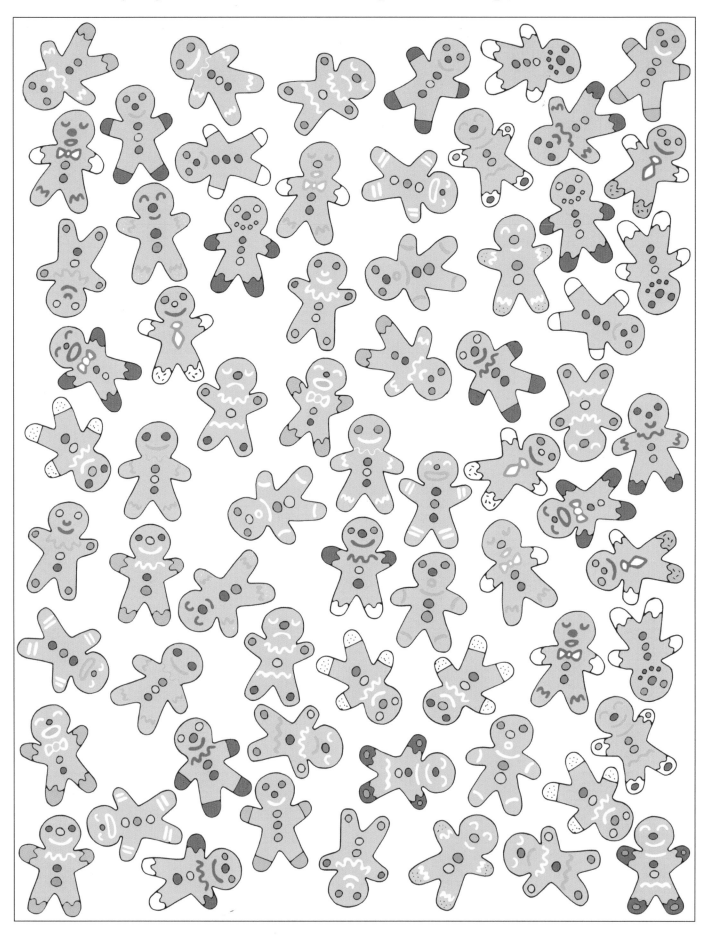

Circle the differences.

It's busy here! Connect the dots, finish the picture, and see why.

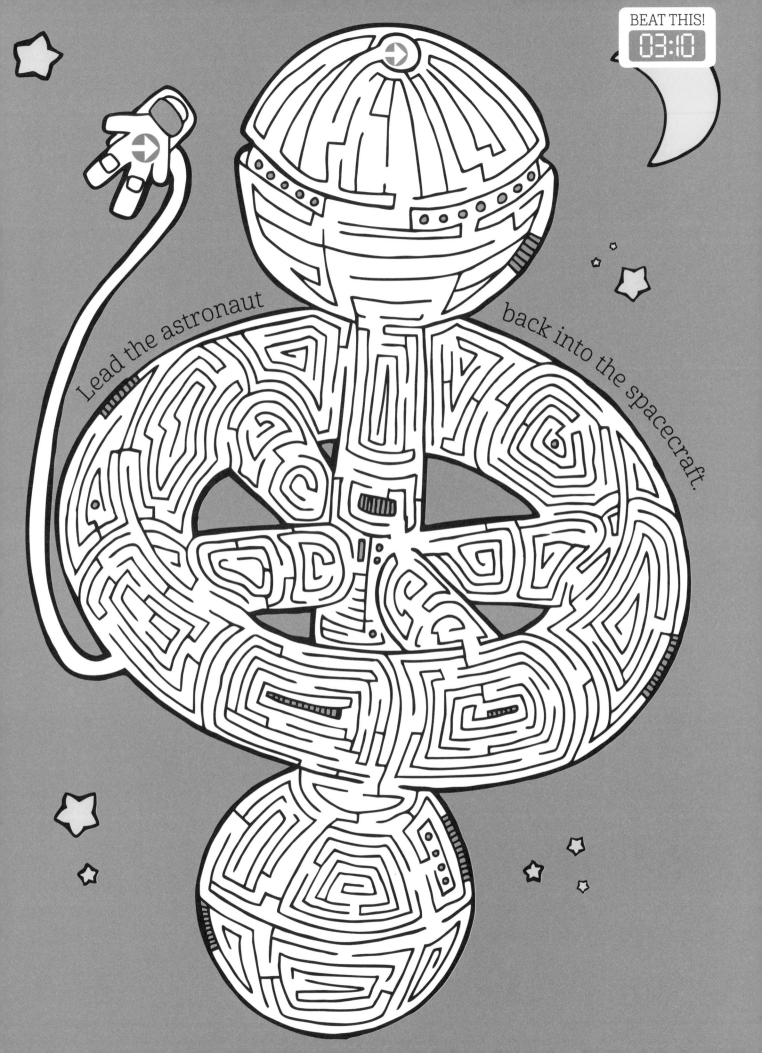

Connect the dots and don't get trapped!

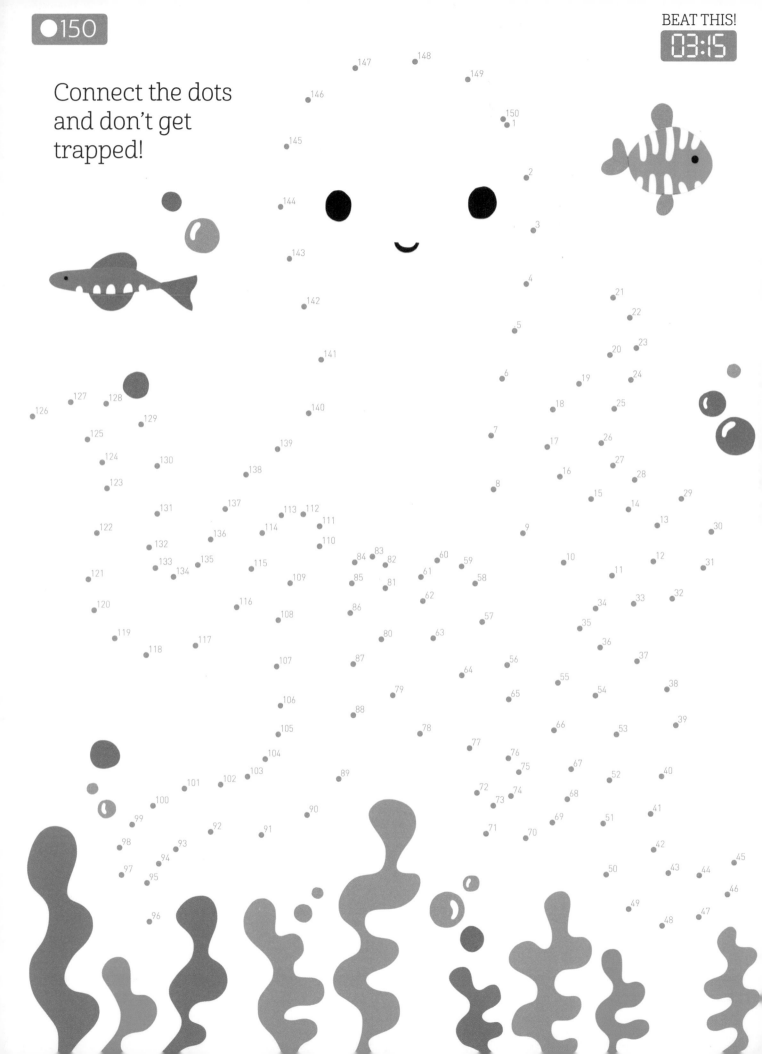

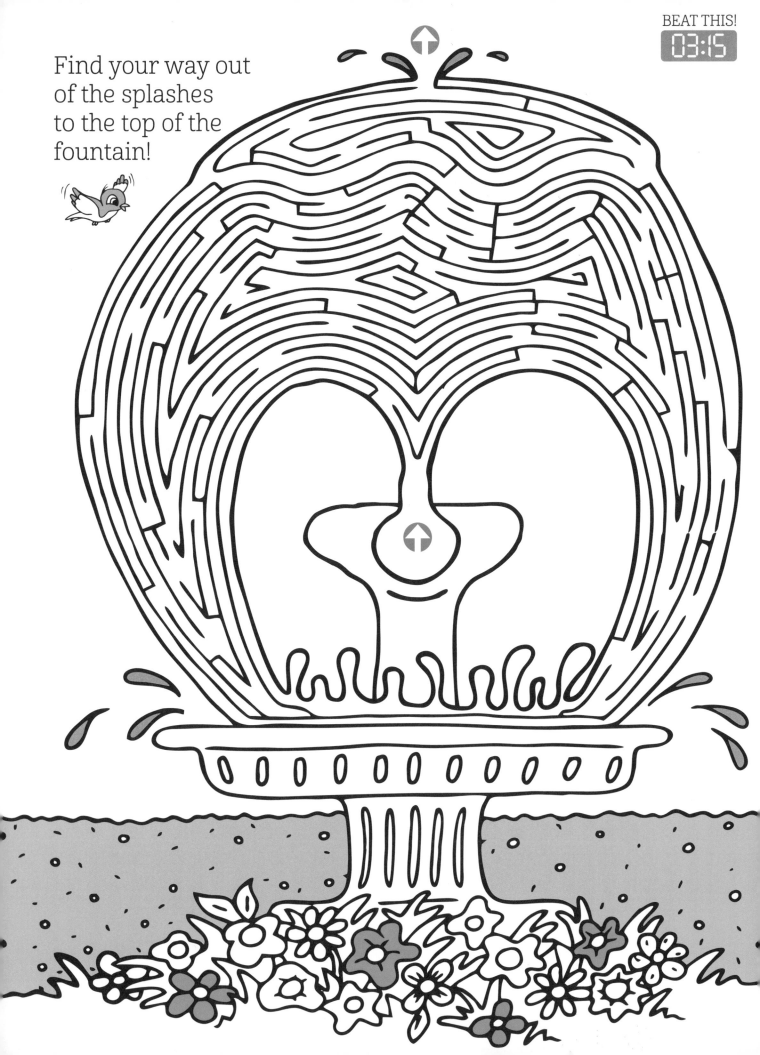

Find your way out of the splashes to the top of the fountain!

Add more stripes when you're done connecting the dots!

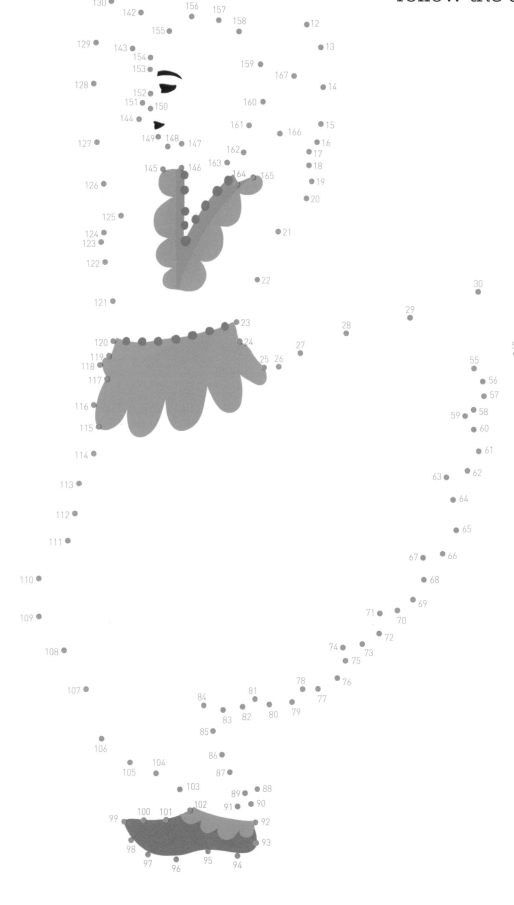

Get in step and
follow the dots!

Can you find your way out of the pattern on the turtle's back and beat the clock?

Come on a dot-
to-dot adventure!

Connect the dots
and add some color!

What game are these guys playing?

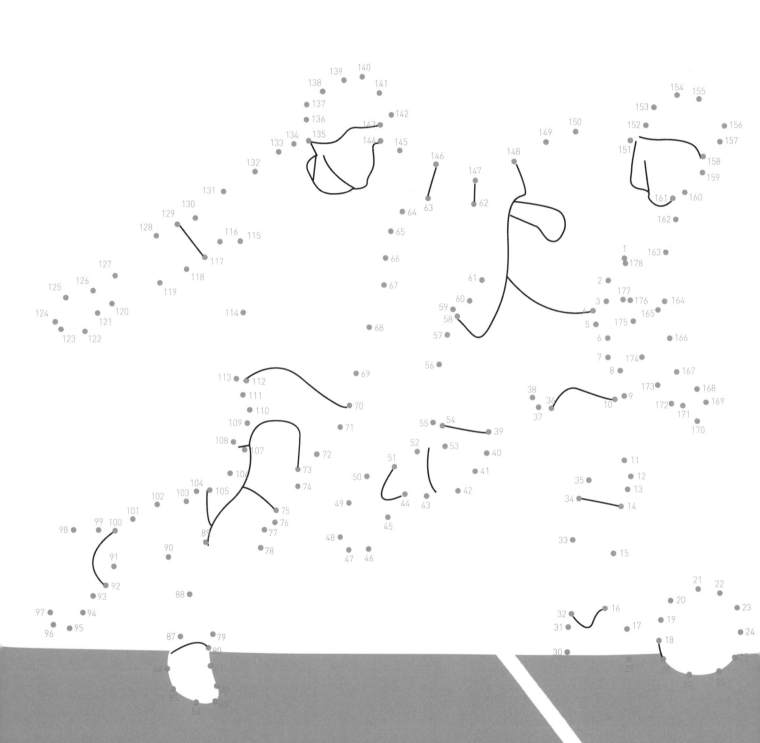

Connect the dots
and add some color!

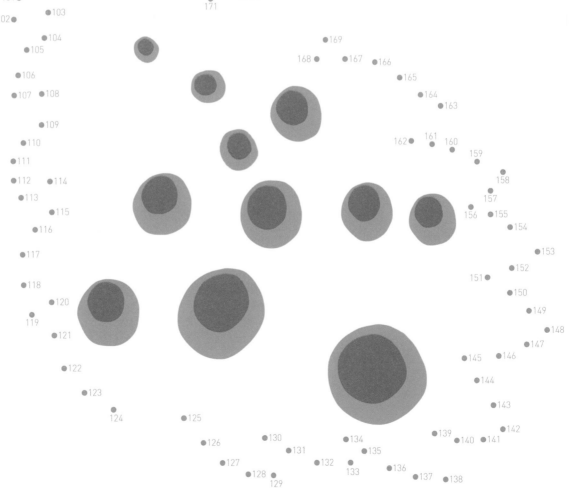

Find these animals hidden in the ocean.

Color in each one you find.

Don't hang around!

These are flags of different countries—except one!

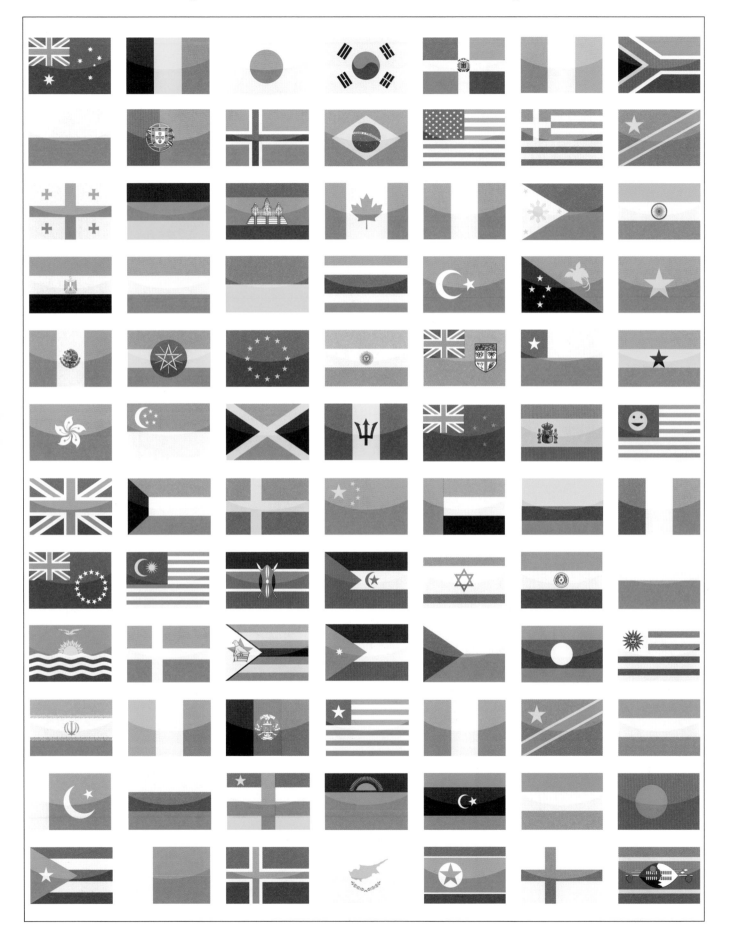

Circle the spooky differences in the drawings.

These don't really exist, but it would be fun to have one! Connect the dots to see this mythical creature.

Connect the dots to spin on the ice!

BEAT THIS!
04:20

Connect the dots and write your own message!

So cute! Connect the dots and add some color.

These lovebugs are all pairs, except for one!

It's very cold here. Where are we?

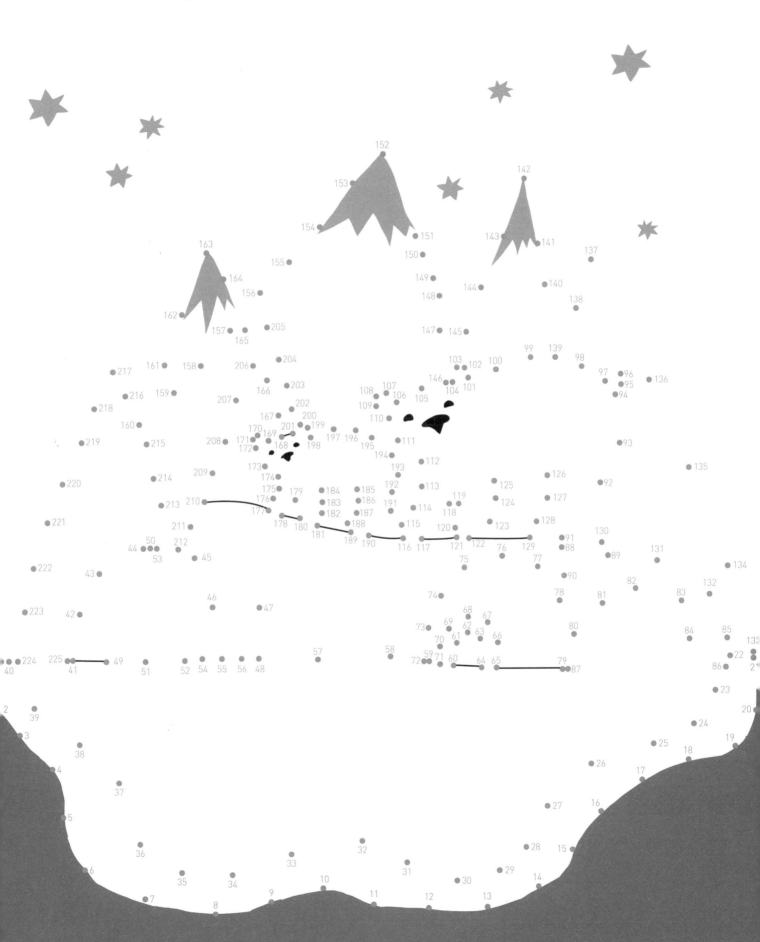

It's cold out there!

This guy needs more color when you're done!

BEAT THIS!
04:50

Find a way through my circuits!

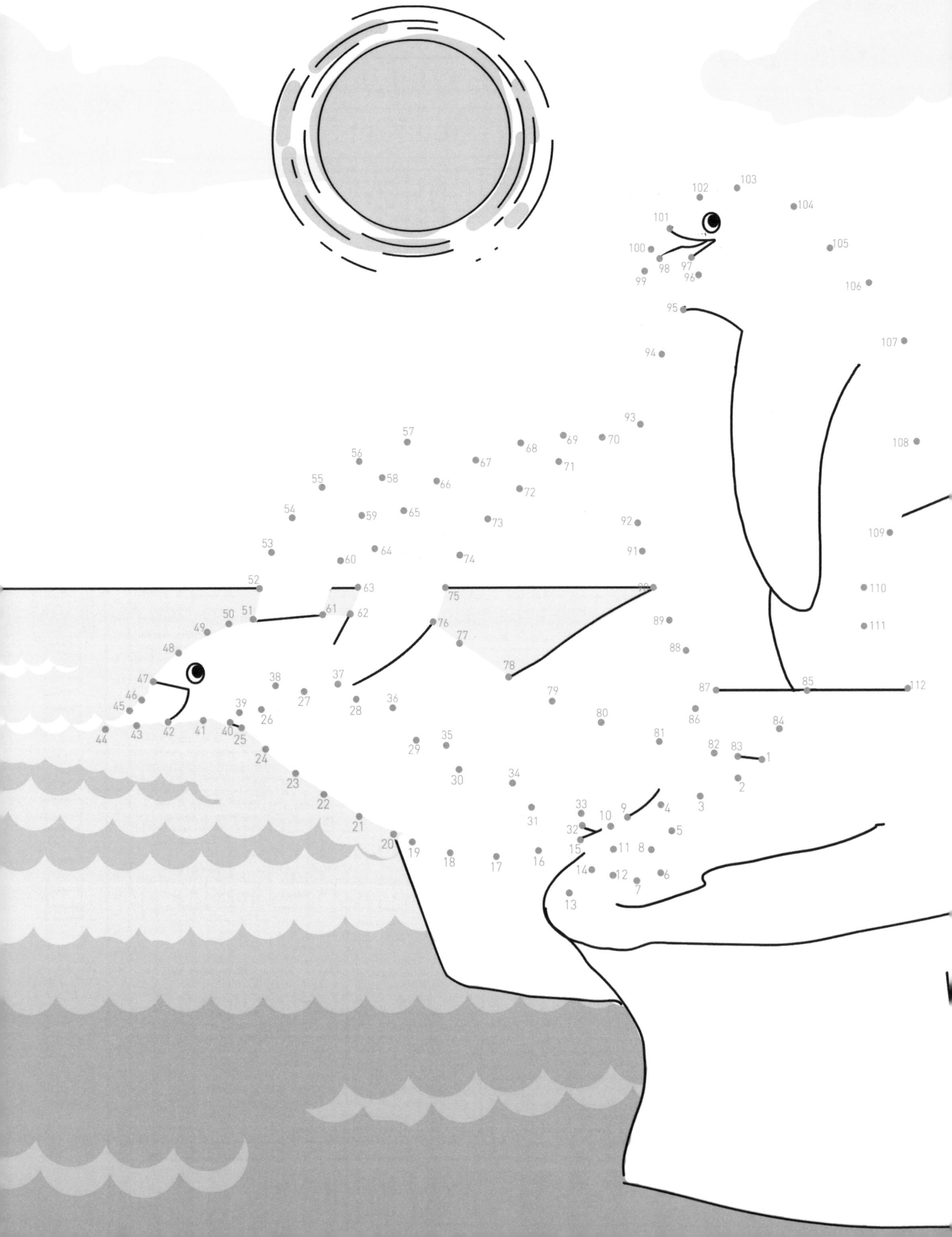

Take your turn and
connect the dots!
Add some color!

Connect the different colored dots and find the creature!

Don't get lost at the first turn!

Connect the dots and color in this cute guy!

Color this animal in gray. Add some
muddy splashes when you're done!

Start on this page.

Find the way to the letter that links up to a letter on the right-hand page and gets you to the end!

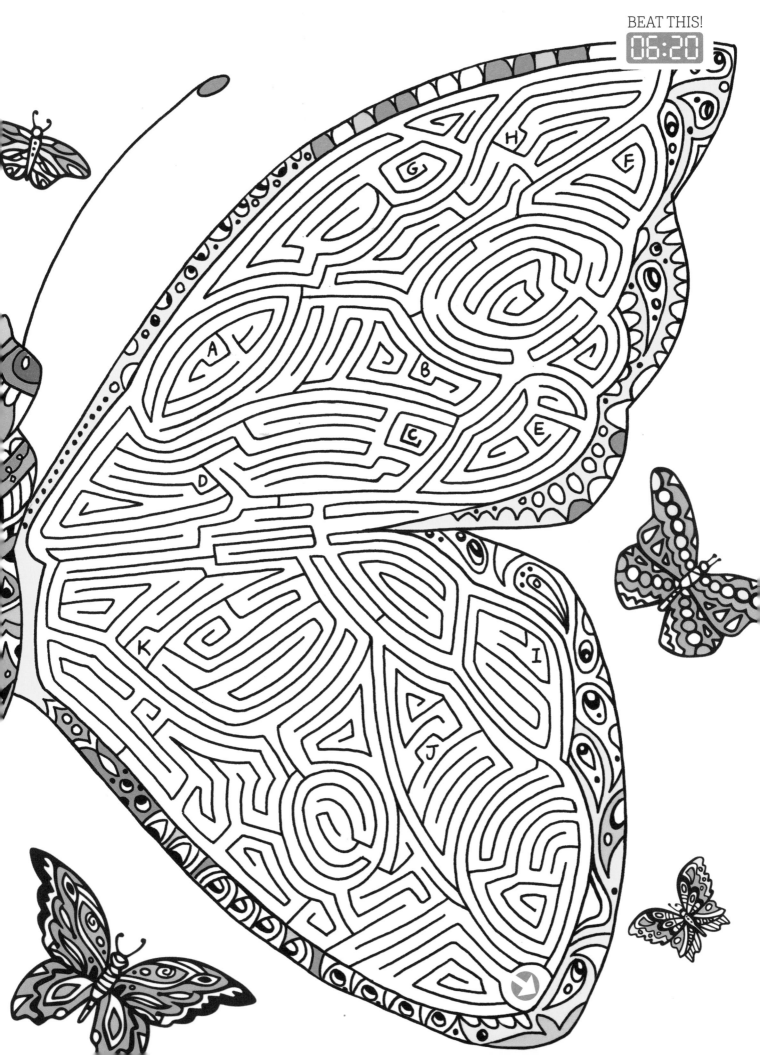

What is this?
Connect the dots to find out.

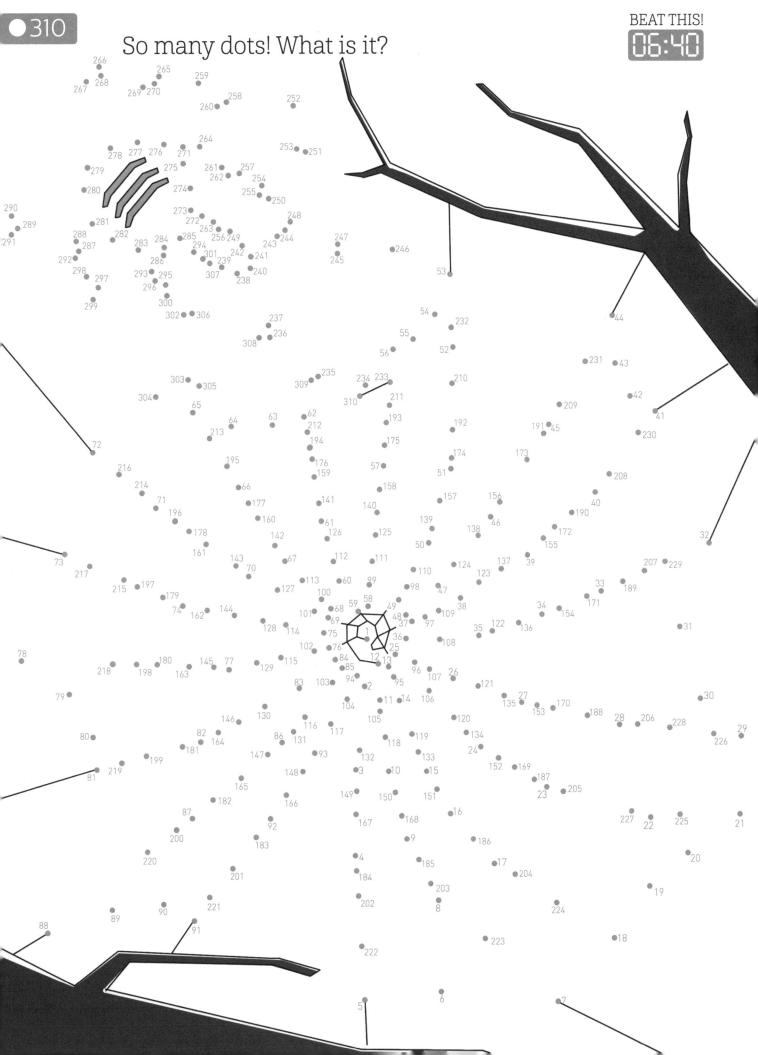

So many dots! What is it?

Connect the dots to find out who we are!

Connect the
different
colored dots.

314

Here's a super city to enjoy!
Connect the different
colored dots.

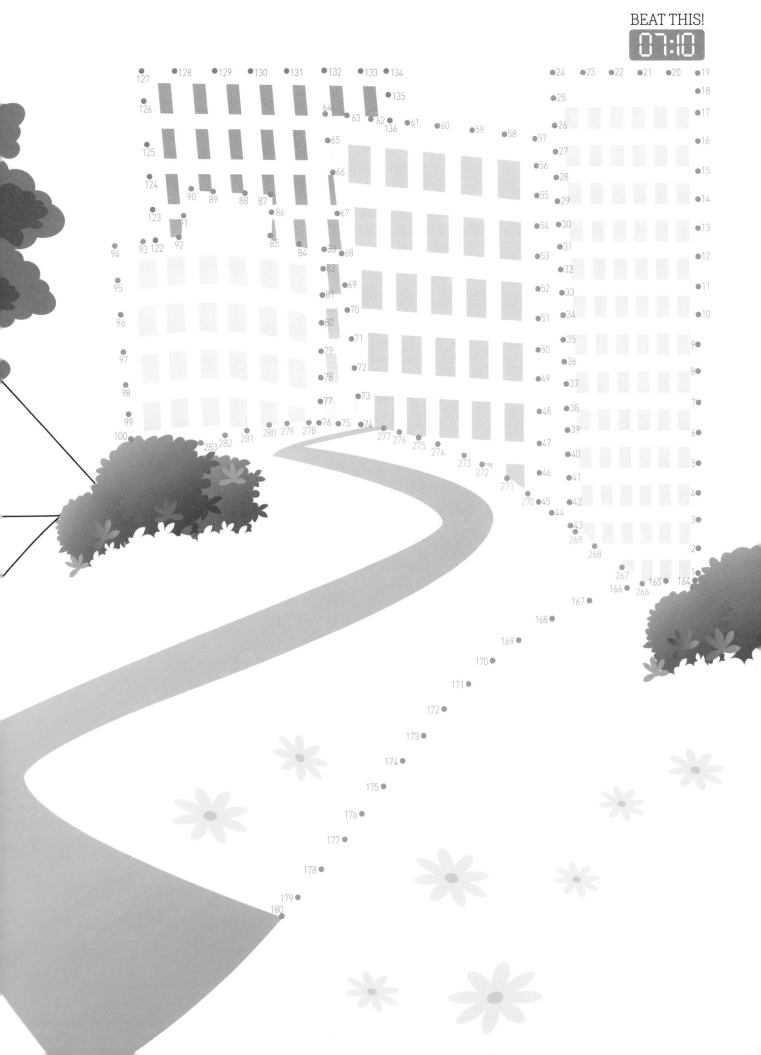

80

Get the diver to the boat by matching the number on this page to the number on the opposite page.

This one is tricky!

Get on board!

Can you copy the picture below to complete the squares?

This one is tricky because it's reversed!

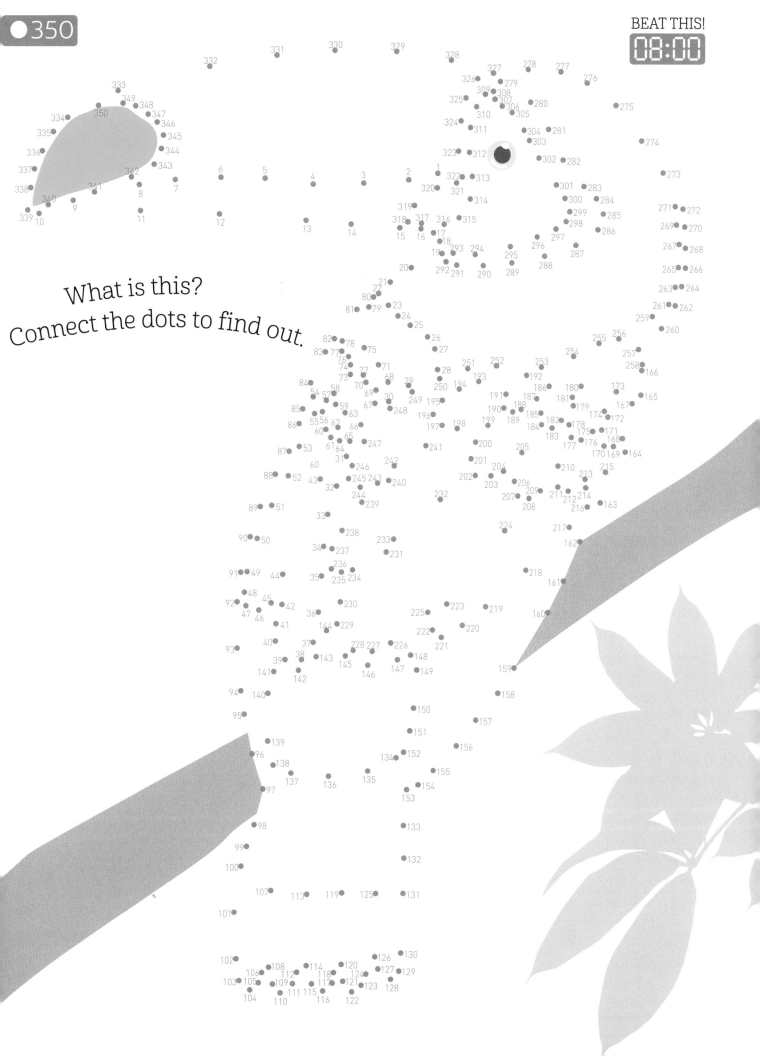

What is this?
Connect the dots to find out.

350

BEAT THIS!
08:00

81

Don't be scared! Connect the dots and color me!

BEAT THIS!
10:00

What is happening here?

●1000

Connect the different colored dots on both pages.

Connect the dots to discover something out of this world!

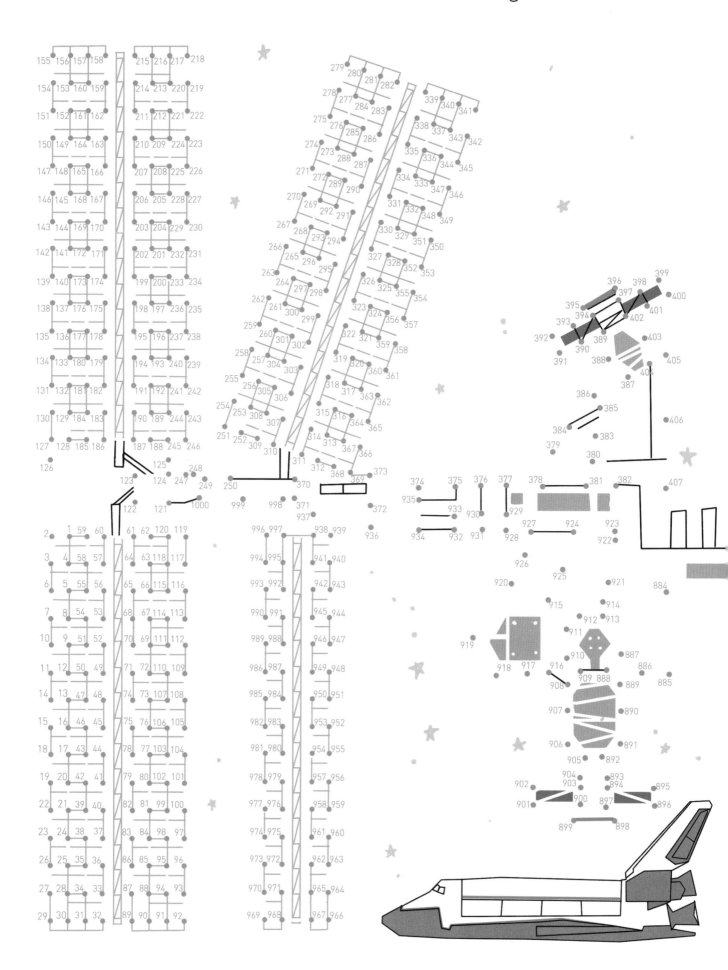

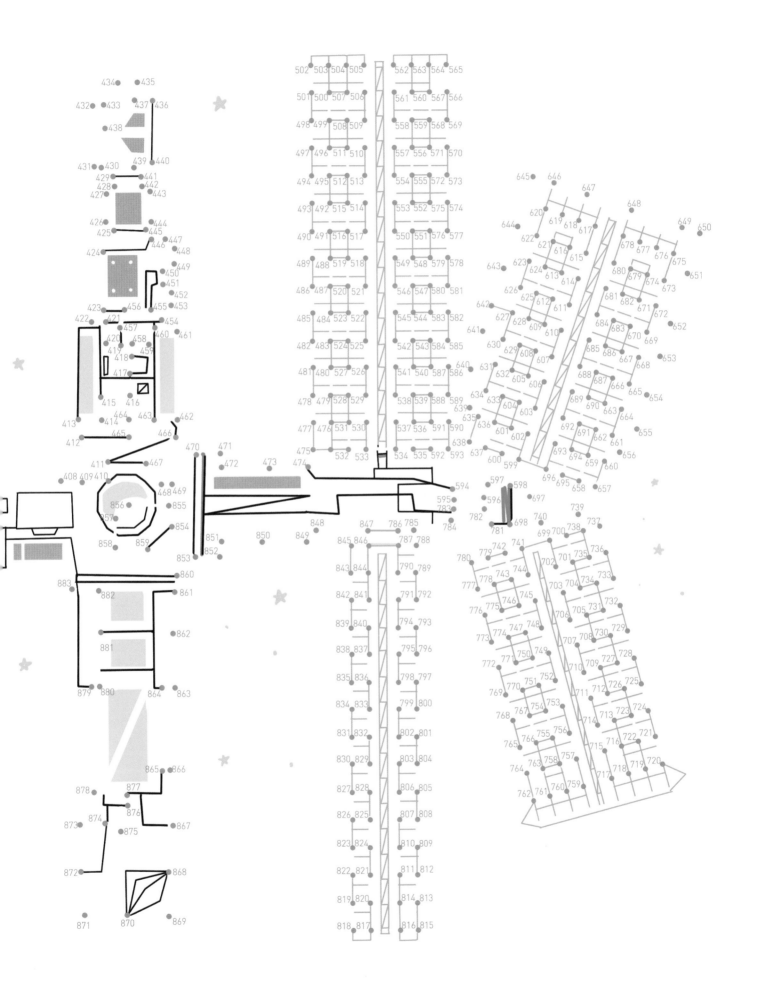

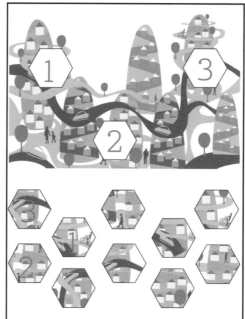
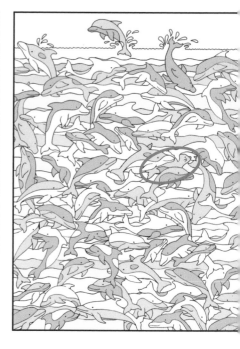

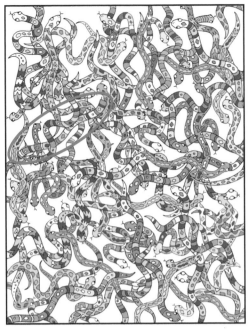

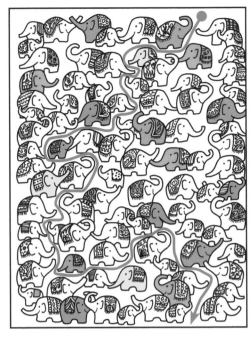

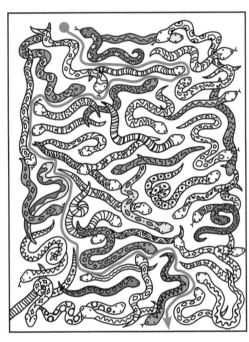

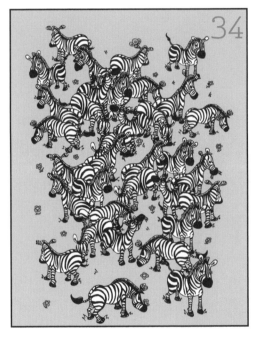

34

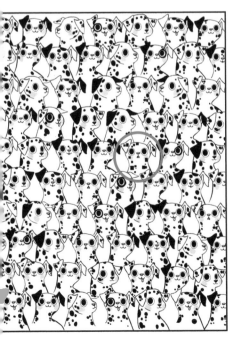

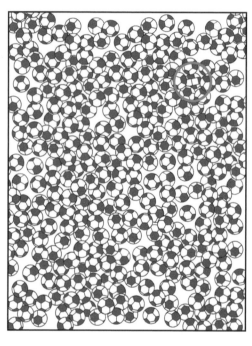

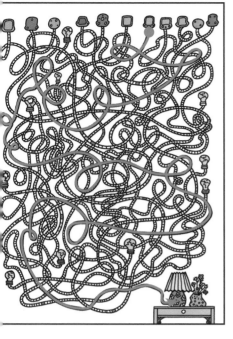

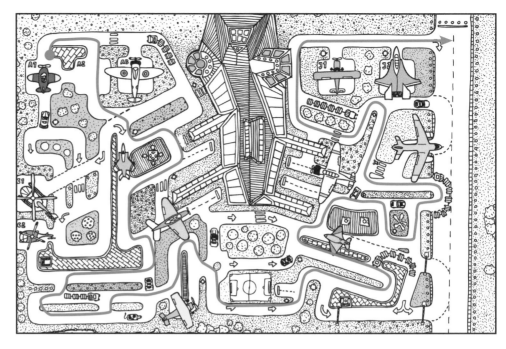

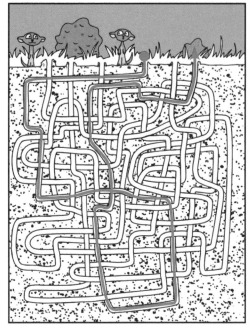

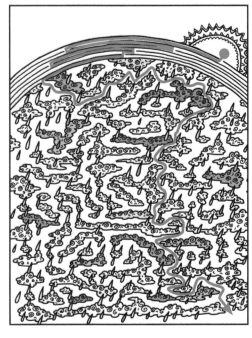
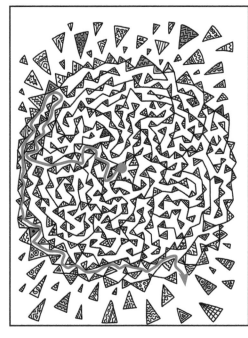
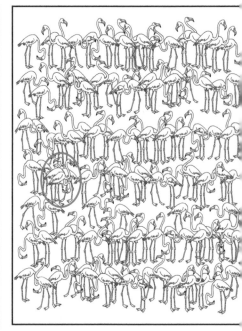
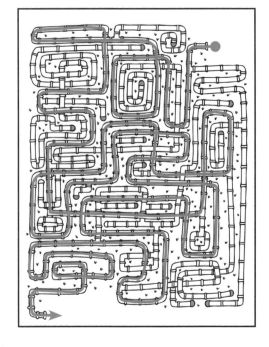
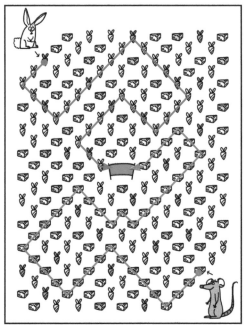

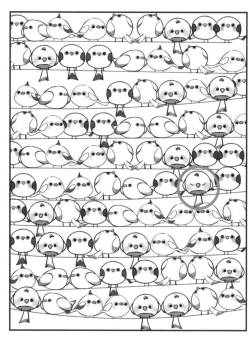

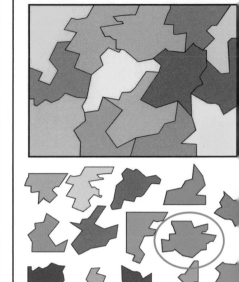

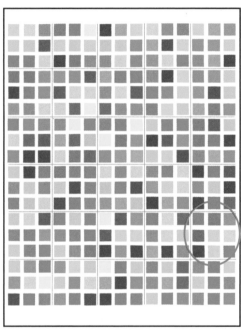

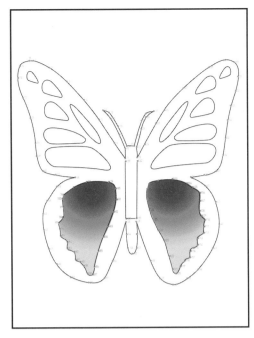

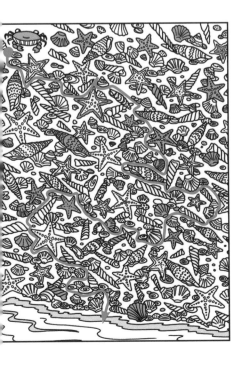

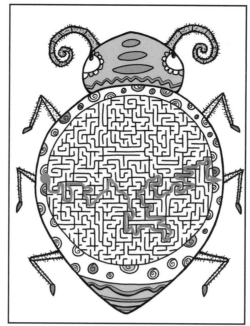

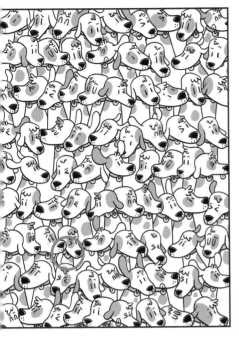

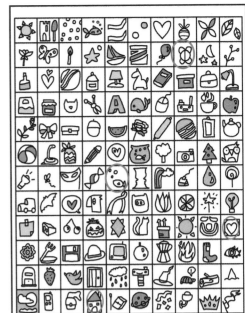

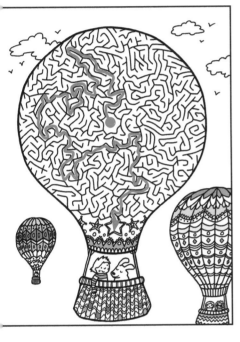

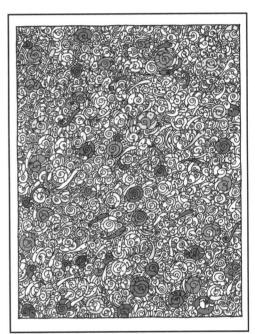

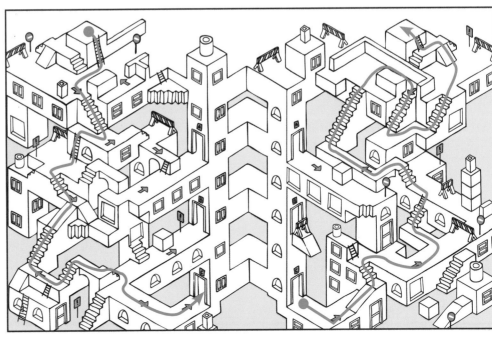

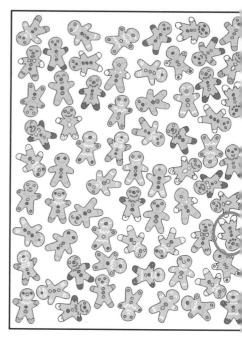

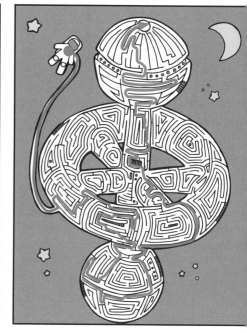

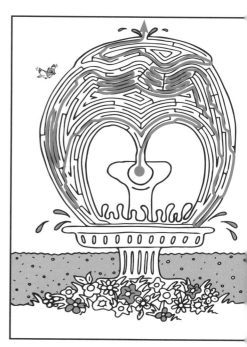

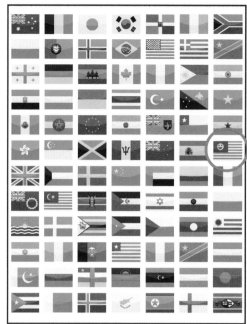

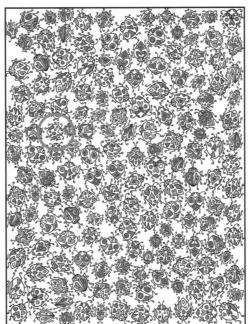

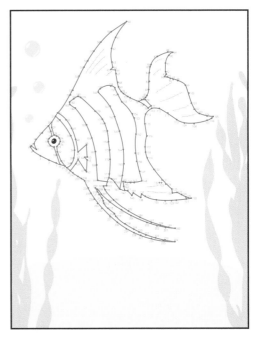

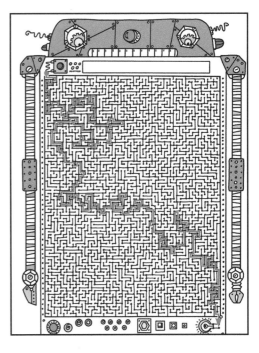

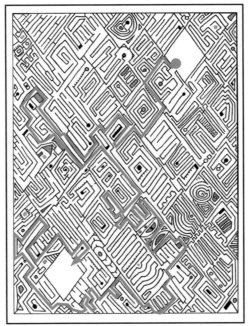

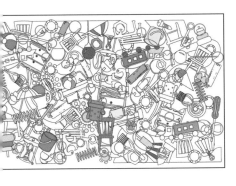

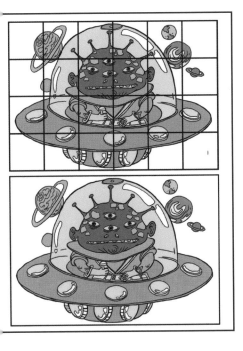

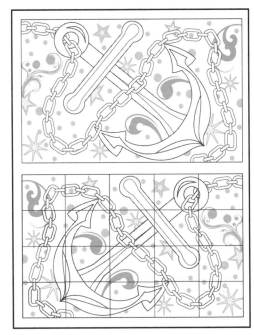

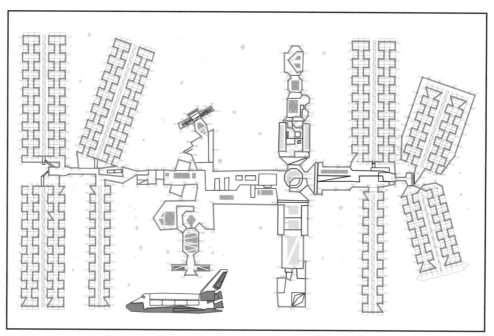